How to Make Shelters

In Survival Situations

I0422027

Prepping and Survival Series

M. Usman

Mendon Cottage Books

JD-Biz Publishing

Disclaimer

The information is this book is provided for informational purposes only. It is not intended to be used and medical advice or a substitute for proper medical treatment by a qualified health care provider. The information is believed to be accurate as presented based on research by the author.

The contents have not been evaluated by the U.S. Food and Drug Administration or any other Government or Health Organization and the contents in this book are not to be used to treat cure or prevent disease.

The author or publisher is not responsible for the use or safety of any diet, procedure or treatment mentioned in this book. The author or publisher is not responsible for errors or omissions that may exist.

Warning

The Book is for informational purposes only and before taking on any diet, treatment or medical procedure, it is recommended to consult with your primary health care provider.

Our books are available at
1. Amazon.com
2. Barnes and Noble
3. Itunes
4. Kobo
5. Smashwords
6. Google Play Books

Table of Contents

Chapter 1: Introduction

A shelter, shade, or house has been a source of protection and comfort for human kind ever since it first realized the benefits of being under a shelter. In many fronts, a shelter is a very fundamental need of living creatures and it has a psychological and emotional importance and value along with physical and material. Men started building shelters in the earliest times of their existence and since then have been developing the most modern and evolutionary methods of building homes with developing and evolving mental models along with advanced technology.

When in the wilderness, shelter is home, a base point to rest, and protection from rain, snow, cold, wild animals, storms, thunders, and sliding lands. Shelter is an unparalleled source of comfort whether you are out in a jungle for an adventure trip or trapped with your friends in an island full of palms and coconuts. Since the primitive ages, creation of shade and formation of a base area to fall upon has been a human norm. The idea of creating a home has nurtured since the beginning of human times on earth, as it was inculcated in man by nature. Creating shelter in the emergency situation can even avoid life threatening situations and provide a point from where the navigation and communication can become easy. Being in possession of the ability and skill set to build a water proof safe shelter is a blessing and drastically increases chances of survival until aid is received. Creating a shade cannot only help protect you from unkind circumstances and adverse situations, but also benefit others who are accompanying you.

Temporary arrangements can also be made by nature if you feel lethargic or have drained yourself with all day tracking. Caves, pits, snow, and dense woods can be your best partners as natural and dependable shelters in cases where building material is not easily available or has been out of reach.

However, such lucky opportunities and not available commonly and that is where people like me start writing such kinds of books. Shelter making is knowledge and an art that we shall discuss in detail through the help of this book. We will explain in detail different ways to create and protect shelters and the material required to accomplish this apparently challenging task.

Location of shelter is very important; you would not want to lie down next to a snake hole. Select an area to build shelter where you can get ample space to lie down flat, comfortably, without apprehensions. Shelter should be developed near the source of building material and water and away from sliding stones, pooling water, and insects. Make your shelter sufficient in size to fit you inside. It should not be very big since it will take more time, material, and effort to construct and should not be so small so that you would need to squeeze yourself to fit in. The best way is to lie down flat and measure your height with the help of a stick or just take a rough measurement with your hands after marking ground from head to toes. Start building your shelter accordingly once you have a good wilderness judgment of your height. A luxury sized shelter is also not advisable because more vacant space inside will not conserve heat and you may feel cold. An effective adventure shade, which is fit enough, will also conserve body heat and would not allow cold to come inside.

Chapter 2: Natural Shelters

All the shelters that are considered most dependable and most comfortable today in survival circumstances are natural shelters which our old ancestors discovered hundreds of thousands of years ago. In this chapter we shall discuss and explain in detail a couple of very popular forms of natural shelters that you can use in survival situations for immediate relief and increased sustainability.

2.1 Shelter from Caves

Pre-historic humans used rocks and caves as permanent living places that protected their possessions including food, water, fire, and other valuables. These days, caves are also destinations to advanced scientific, geological, or anthropological studies as well as picnic and adventure trips intended for exploration and entertainment.

Step 1: Rock Selection

Before selecting the cave to lie in, it is important to ensure that pieces and parts of the rock do not tend to fall or break. Select a strong and firm rock that is dry and has relatively less humidity. Caves which are wet and humid are more likely to be the home of wild animals and reptiles and it may not be a good idea to trust them as hosts. Dry rocks also stay warm and are a good receptive of heat from fire that you may need to create alongside to maintain survival temperature and hush away predators.

Edges and hanging rocks on the roof of your cave home are acceptable and manageable as long as the height of cave is enough to fit you inside while standing. Otherwise, a small misjudgment on the height part can hurt you. Try avoiding flat caves where you cannot enter unless creeping alongside the ground. Find a cave where you can enter at least after slight bending.

Step 2: Preparing the Bed

A bed inside the rock should be created after cleaning the surface of flints, stones, and small sharp pieces of rocks. Once the cleaning is done and you find a nice, smooth, and flat surface to extend your bed, have a detailed review of the surroundings to assure that there are no slits or openings around to allow rain water to come inside and the place is perfectly dry. Also, assure that it is positioned inside the rock and near the opening in a fashion that allows fire heat to warm you and protect you. The bed should not be deep in a pit or depression and should the highest place of the cave surface. A good bed is made of dry leaves, bushes, shrub, hay, and small tree branches of soft wood like bough. A bug free bed is preferably a little higher than ground level. However, it is a challenging task to build a bed which is above ground from survival material. If you were smart enough to take cord, rope, or weaving material and are lucky enough to find long, strong, and firm branches of trees to build a grid structure for your survival bed, you can get a bed which is higher than ground to protect you from bugs and reptiles. If your fire is positioned strategically and it is assured, before selecting the rock and preparing the bed, that your neighborhood is clear of reptiles and bugs then go ahead.

2.2 Snow Caves and Shelters

Certain conditions may warrant immediate refuge against threats to survival where the decision making is required smartly and without losing much time. In a survival situation, having a shelter can make the difference of life and death, and natural choices of shelters can be utilized to readily achieve this difference.

Snow caves or snow shelters are mostly used by mountain climbers and hikers and have proven to be very effective to protect against extreme temperatures, precipitation, and wild animals. A snow cave made with proper methodology in mind can help maintain an inside temperature of $0°$ when it is chilling outside at $-30°$. Digging and developing snow caves is not an easy task and efforts may remain futile without accurate method and tools. This is the reason most of the climbers take ditch digging material along with warm jackets to keep themselves protected and warm inside snow. We are going to discuss and explain a commonly used method of developing a snow shelter in situations and circumstances allowing it.

Step 1: Check your instruments and clothing before starting to shovel a cave for you in the snowy wilderness. For this method to be successful, one has to be in possession of a compact and convenient snow shovel and a torch or some other source of light for use in the night.

Step 2: Find an area which is risk free in terms of snow slides, avalanche, or rock fall. Most hikers avoid sloppy areas with deep snow at altitudes higher than the spot selected for shelter. Always remember that snow clogging can suffocate and kill you if you are confined airless inside your snow home. Make sure that the opening or hole of your cave is clear and away from heaps of snow. If possible, clear away some snow from the "door" to get an easy escape way in an emergency evacuation.

Step 3: Select snow which is hard and avoid snow which is light and dusty in looks. Make sure it is somewhere against the direction of slope and pile up the snow so that you can dig up to 3 to 5 ft. deep.

Step 4: Measure piled up snow to calculate if the required number of people will easily fit inside if you dig it into a cave. Also keep in mind the physique and height of the people going to reside inside the cave. Ideally, a 5 feet tall pile should be enough for 2 people to sit and lie down inside. The snow heap should be firmly packed and appear solid to assure safety and longevity. Stomping the snow with a board, the spine of your shove, or your shoe sole is a good option to pack and firm the snow heap.

Step 5: Wait for at least two hours to let the cold breeze freeze out your new home and make it strong enough so that it doesn't collapse on you. Don't starting shoving dry and powdery snow as this will always have the risk of falling down into pieces.

Step 6: Shove off the snow from the bottom and create a hollow center of the pile. Once enough room is created, you can go inside and adjust the snow with your feet to make your body fit inside as per your convenience. Cold air would not enter your new room if the floor of the cave is higher than the entrance as this will stop the cold breeze at your door.

Step 7: For the purpose of finishing, carve in the walls and roof to create a sufficient comfortable room and rule out the dripping of cold water from the bumps of the walls and ceiling. Also, place a ski pole on top of the cave and mark the edges with brightly colored gear or whatever you can find. It is advisable to create ventilation holes to allow air inside and avert suffocation.

A snow cave formed after piling up the snow heap and then excavating the inside room is called "Quinzhee". While igloo is used for seasonal habitation, quinzhees are more popular with adventurists and campers or built for survival purposes.

Chapter 3: Wood Shelters

Shelters are your best friends in the woods and first priority to build once we are out in the middle of a rough weather or terrain. Shelters do not only protect us from rain, snow, wind, and extreme temperatures, but also enable us to hide from life threatening objects, situations, and predators.

This chapter is more about extreme raw and man-made shelters built and maintained in hand crafted style in the Rocky Mountains, while shivering in the freezing breeze or in the middle of the dark woods.

3.1 The Dome Shelters

Dome style shelters are based on wigwam structure, and are developed with the help of everything you can find in the tough situation. It doesn't actually mean that you can use anything you find in your way, but a selected list of ingredients which you can likely find in areas one might be struck in and call for rescue. The main ingredients of dome style shelters are:

1.   Leaves, bough, bushes, and limbs for bed.

2.   At least 6 firm and straight limbs and logs for structure.

3.   Small saplings or firm straight sticks for structure of the bed

4.   Branch tips or green bough are a great option for bed mattress.

Step 1: Build the frame by placing four 8 ft long and ½ ft in diameter wood limbs stacked over each other. The limbs are separated by 2 logs or brackets at least 3-5 ft in length, depending on the width of shelter required, crossed at head side and foot side each, as shown in the picture.

Step 2: Make sure that at least 1 ft tall support is present at the bottom of your structure to prevent your body heat from absorbing into the earth and to protect you from worms and bugs. Take wood brackets or wood pieces on which you can firmly place your log structure and tie the knots on all four sides. Try lashing rope or wire in knotting form which joins the frame and support and is strong enough to absorb body movement.

Step 3: When the structure is already in place and the bed is also prepared with the help of soft saplings heaped nicely in a herringbone pattern (my favorite for home like comfort), then the next step is to create a dome. Take 6 to 10 soft and flexible sticks or saplings and cut them to same size that should be 8 ft in length and 1 inch in diameter. Remember that our floor and bed structure is also made from the same length pieces of trees. Try cane like saplings for creating a dome roof.

Step 4: Stick these saplings in the ground on both sides or wedge them with the edges of the frame and let them curve over the structure to form a wigwam dome roof. Remember that when you are bending and fixing the saplings on the head and foot of your structure, distance them equally and avoid using ropes to tie them on sides.

Step 5: Take further 4-8 saplings and weave them on the back side to create a wall behind you. Now your half dome structure is ready.

In a case where the given input material is available, the total time consumed in building this dome like shelter should not be more than one hour. You would need an axe, knife, or any other sharp edged object to cut the wood pieces, saplings, and wooden brackets and to adjust the sizes or smooth the edges to make the sticks and clubs straight in shape. You can cover your dome with plastic to pack the roof to protect from rain and snow.

3.2 Ramada Shelters

Ramada shelters are completed with mat or tarp roofs and are best for sunny and hot environments that offer shade from the sun and remains open from all four sides. A Ramada is a partially closed temporary shelter commonly used in southwestern America and is good for climates and circumstances where protection from heat is necessary for survival. However, it doesn't provide protection from rain or snow, as Ramada shelters have no walls on either of the sides. We will briefly explain the material used and steps required to create this good looking shelter.

Step 1: Find at least 4 – 8 thick beams of the wood that will be the structure pillars of your Ramada shelter. These can be cut and trimmed in size and are easy to find if you are near a country side or lost somewhere in the woods. The heights of the beams have to be a little taller than the tallest person who is out with you.

Step 2: Erect the 4 pillars like the pillars of your room. Dig 4 small holes, keeping in mind the width and length coordinates of your Ramada, and insert 4 beams in these holes deep enough so that the bottom of the beam fixes inside to erect without any other support.

Step 3: Support the structure by crossing the 4 pillars in a diagonal shape, cutting each other with 2 on each side. These diagonal pillar walls should be placed on two sides as walls to protect the roof of your structure.

Step 4: Weave and cross the ceiling material that we collected on the way, to form insulting cheddar to work as the roof of your Ramada. In case we have a large piece of cloth or tarp available, it is going to the best choice as long as it protects us from rain and heat.

Step 5: Lift the roof sheet from the corners one by one and tie the knots in circles with each pillar. Try creating holes for loops to hang around the pillars. You can use wires or plastic cords to loop around the holes and fix the sheet on pillars. Stay safe inside!

3.3 Teepee/Tipi

A Teepee or Tipi is tent style tropical shelter for temporary adventure or survival use, and it is good for protection from extreme temperatures as well as house fire. It is a very comfortable, durable, and relatively easy to make structure which is popular with trackers, adventurers, and mountain hikers. Unlike other wood based shelters, a tipi is mobile and an easily transferable structure and we can move a tipi from one place to another in search of emergency rescue. Let's dive into the knowledge of material and knowledge needed to create a tipi.

Step 1: Get hold of canvas which is 15x30 ft in coordinates; traditionally they used animal skins like ones peeled off from buffalos. However, since now buffalo skins are not easily available, canvas is a good option as an alternative.

Step 2: We can use lodge poles or canes to structure our tipi which can firmly fix in structure and support the canvas. Scrap and smooth the sturdy 12 poles with a knife or sandpaper.

Step 3: Prepare and cut your canvas for the tipi and cut a semi-circle symmetric in width and length in terms of size. Cut two notches on each side of the semi-circle and cut two flaps right around the middle of the flat side.

Step 4: For knotting and tying the joints and connecting the structure frame, get manila or straw rope long enough to complete all the knots appropriately.

Step 5: Erect the tripod by laying two poles together on the ground and placing the third one diagonally over the two poles, at 30 degree angle. The two base poles should face towards the center of the flat side of the canvas. Tie these three poles with your straw rope, preferably using clove-hitch, and do not detach or cut the remaining rope as this will come in handy later in the next step. This joint is roughly at 1/3rd distance from the top of the poles.

Step 6: Place poles on sides around the tripod, making a circle, and leave some place for the lift pole which is going to be in the center of the circle. Leave space for the door when placing a circle of poles and, if required, spare a big sheet of canvas for shutting the door opening and closing for unwarranted creatures.

Step 7: Tie all the poles, including the central support pole, by walking around your tipi structure holding the rope that we left uncut in an earlier step. The rope should cross all the joints and the leftover rope should hang around the corner.

Step 8: Roll the edges of the canvas alongside the poles, lift it in the air and then unroll the canvas neatly, covering up your structure with it. Fix the gap that you had left in the middle of the canvas in your central support pole, also called lift pole earlier, in a way so that the lift pole pops out of the canvas in the center.

Step 9: Once the frame of poles is covered by the canvas wrap, it should start looking good. Make sure you have left the door opening uncovered and then the final stage begins. Pin the flaps of canvas on the ground with nail like objects you can find easily, so that the wrap doesn't fall itself and wind doesn't disturb it.

You can create smoke flaps or openings on the side walls of the canvas if you plan to start a fire inside. However, your fire bed should be centrally placed away from canvas walls.

Chapter 4: Tarp Shelters

In literal terms, a tarp is the name of any sheet or cover that is used to insulate an area in order to safeguard against extreme natural elements like scorching sunlight, rain, or snow. Tarp can be made of plastic sheets, animal skins, large clothing materials, or any other insulating materials which do not allow the above stated elements to pass through them. Tarp shelters are also categorized as easy to build and reliable shades best used in natural settings. Let's have a brief list of items you will need to create them.

1.   A long cord or ridgeline.

2.   Two pieces of poles or beams at least 10 ft. tall if you are in area scarce of trees.

3.   A tent tarp fabricated from insulating material.

The best starting point for creating a tarp based shelter is to find a couple of trees parallel to each other with at least 10 ft height and separated from each other to the extent the available length of your cord or rope can afford. The distance between the two points will determine enlarged covering area of your shelter. Let's go step by step now:

Step 1: Using a bowline knot, tie the rope with two trees or poles, at height which is little higher than your shoulder. Select an area which is shy of strong winds as tarps are very vulnerable to wind. Make this ridgeline as tight as possible as your shelter's firmness will be directly derived from sturdiness of the rope.

Step 2: Readymade tarps have loops created on the corner points that you can use to tie your ropes. However, if you are using a piece of cloth, shade, or any other material, you will need to create four holes on each corner. Preferably the shade will be thick and opaque and square or rectangle in shape.

Step 3: Loop the cords on the edge of the tarp; if possible, use a taut line hitch or loop at one side to link in the cord so that it is easy to move or slide the tarp when required.

Step 4: Pin down the edges of tarp on the ground using the cord that you looped on the edges. The stakes at the corner should create a 45° angle with the ground and once pulled tight, the tarp should look like an open tent shaped as a hut. Pull the sides and corners tights to make the cloth or shade free of wrinkles and creases. Use tent stakes to nail down the tarp to the ground; in cases where tent stakes are not available you may use large rocks or firm limbs to secure the tarp along the ground.

Step 5: Fix your shelter to adjust the weather and you have already left the margin by riding the rope or cord on the baseline formed as a ridgeline connected by two trees. For example in warmer climates, you can lift up the tarp to allow air inside.

Chapter 5: Debris Hut

A debris hut is a natural emergency refuge, in shell or trap form, which is deemed one the easiest and convenient overhead shades to seek as protection. In the basic definition of shelter, it is made of organic wood side debris consisting of bough, leaf litter, bushes, and tree spur. We are going to review the steps and materials required to develop a debris hut hereby. However, you shall remain flexible with material as a debris hut is based on individual architecture techniques and there are no rules.

Step 1: Locate and pile as big an amount of debris and duff material as you can find. You can get hold of torn or dry branches of trees, weathered leaves, and battered dough.

Step 2: To minimize air circulation on a cold day or night, always close doorways. This will help maintain body temperature inside and in cases where you have arranged fire inside, the closed door shelters create nice warm temperature and ambiance to enjoy your self-cooked dinner.

Step 3: Create a ditch or pocket which should be 6-8 inches deep. Stub and pack the floor of this ditch to create bed and you can do this by crawling down the pocket and adjusting the surface with your hand or feet.

Step 4: Get 3 blocks of ridgepoles and slice them to fit on the support of your tripod shaped pole or set of poles that you have already pinned on the ground. Your tripod support can also be a growing tree which has a base tall enough with emerging tripod shape, to lay your ridgepole.

Step 5: Weave and fabricate the debris, pine needles, bough, or slabs of bark that we collected in step 1 to create cheddar of debris to work as a roof and walls.

Step 6: Lace the ridgepoles with your support tripod and tilt them to make an upright structure. In order to create an A-frame roof and walls, lift the cheddar from the front and place it as crotch with the tripod branch.

Closed shelters take more time and effort than open shelters, but the return and reward of these shelters are double than the sweat to make them. A debris hut may not sound that easy and convenient to you, but in literal terms the catch here is just finding or creating a tripod style root or bud of tree. The remaining material can be substituted with any solid ingredients for cheddar or pillar that you can find with the least energy consumed.

On the other hand tipi structures are famously used from primitive times, especially by nomadic tribes and travelling hunters. Enclosed tipis take 3-4 hours to make in the wilderness conditions and facilitate protection from snow and rain. You can enjoy firelight illumination inside if ample ventilation is allowed and safety measures are taken care of, including having a basket of water close by.

Chapter 6: Conclusion

Developing a shelter is one of the most sought after outdoor crafts required for safeguarding from unwarranted elements and sustaining for the longer period of time in order to survive, before aid is within access. Shelters connect to humans physically and emotionally as they provide a sense of security and create a home-like feeling. The following are a few basic factors which should be kept in mind before going out for adventures that may call for building shelters on your own:

6.1 Factors

1. **Location:** Choose a dry, flat, and safe location where water, food, and building material sources are nearby. Avoid locations that may endanger you from land-sliding, snow avalanche, nests of dangerous reptiles, or falling branches. Location should be selected in context where the flat floor of the shelter allows abundant are to lie down.

2. **Structure:** All our survival shelters are built to protect us from the unforeseen therefore their architecture should organically protect us from the dangerous elements in surrounding as well as themselves. Use firm and strong branches to support the structure and framework and avoid the material which looks faltering or limp.

3. **Size:** Calculation of size of the room and internal area of the shelter is very a sensitive area and sometimes beginners make them too large or too small. Apart from an educated guess, the best solution is to go inside the shade when you are developing it and try different postures in standing tall and lying flat to ensure that you will remain comfortable and don't hit the walls and ceiling of the shelter while you are present inside. Also, the vacant space inside should be on a

minimum level to conserve body heat and allow minimum cold air inside.

4. **Heating Sources:** While many structures and models have fire and smoke holes built, it is not always safe to have fire inside. Since most of the structures are based out of wood and other flammable materials, the fire source should be placed away from the structure and preferably set in the center. Rely on body heat and insulate your shelter as much as possible so that you don't need to set fire inside. Even if you start fire, collect substantial firewood and take utmost care so that you don't burn your shelter.

5. **Shelter Cover:** Animal skins, leather, bough/debris sheets, or plastic are favorite covers over your shelters to keep away rain, snow, wind, and extreme temperatures. As discussed in above methods, leaves, dry grass, wood saplings, and ferns should be properly weaved and toiled to lash over the structure firmly in order to insulate your new home. Leave a ventilation notch especially if you plan to light a fire inside.

If you diverged on the mountain side and cannot find your way back to the highway, first look for easiest ways to cover yourself. Alternative ways to shade and protect you can be:

1. Finding a fallen tree or dense branches and spending a night starring at stars (if it is clean out there).

2. Finding and getting inside a cave or huge rock

When it comes to the structure of shelter, there are three crucial factors that we need to keep in mind before beginning. Size, safety, and material are the most crucial elements to consider at the time of architecture and design discussions. The structure of your emergency shelter heavily depends on size, safety, and available material and in any case you would want to make it simple, safe, and constructible fast with the least effort, with the help of conveniently available material. Large and strong branches can be building blocks of a strong and safe shelter. One will always have to cut, carve, and shape the branches in multiple ways and forms so that they fix with each other firm and at least tolerate the weight of an adult.

Without cover or insulation, a shelter will not bring you all the benefits that are deemed to be provided by every basic shelter. You will need to cover the roof of your shelter at least to be protected from sunlight, rain, snow, or wind. Debris like leaves, bushes, dry grass, stick, and ferns should be used to cover your shelter from the top and preferably from the side walls too. To protect yourself from breeze or cold, the best option is to create insulation of soil or dust or even bark if you can get hold of some. Your inside bed should also be constructed from this menu of debris in order to protect you from cold.

Regardless of the scenario and extent of emergency you may face, it is very important to remain calm and remain in control. Getting anxious and being in a panicked state will push you to make wrong decisions, while keeping in control of your emotions and being in right frame of mind may create the difference of life and death depending upon the situation. Basic shelters are overwhelmingly useful to sustain and survive from harsh outdoor factors. Practice your favorite shelter making techniques before planning your next excursion.

Author Bio

Muhammad Usman is a distinguished medical graduate of Allama Iqbal medical college (AIMC). He is a professional writer who has been in the field for more than 4 years. During this time he has produced 10,000+ articles, blogs and eBooks on various niches related to diseases, health, fitness, nutrition and well-being. He is a regular contributor to several journals related to medicine and surgery. He is the editor of several journals and newspapers.

Check out some of the other JD-Biz Publishing books

Gardening Series on Amazon

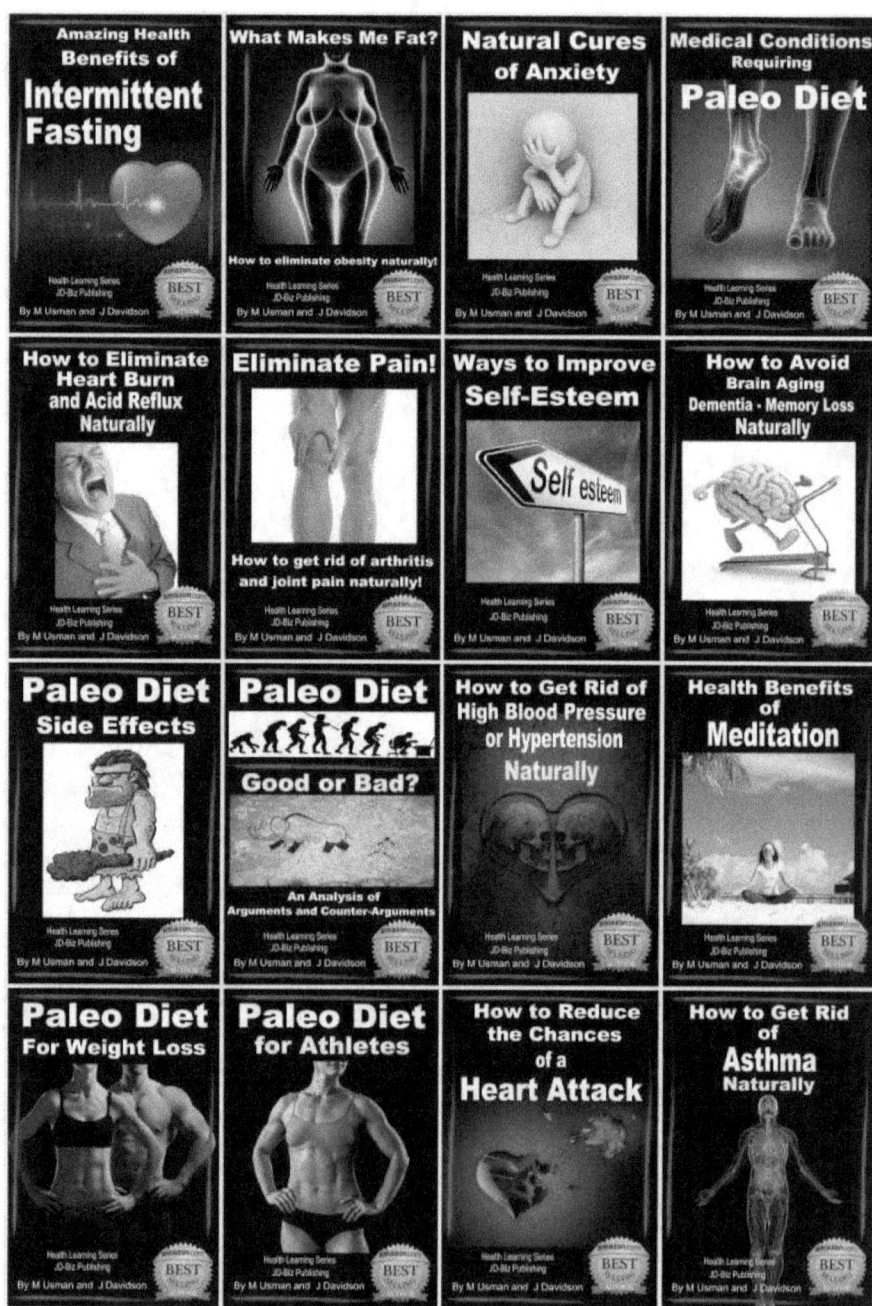

Amazing Animal Book Series

Learn To Draw Series

How to Build and Plan Books

Entrepreneur Book Series

Our books are available at

1. Amazon.com

2. Barnes and Noble

3. Itunes

4. Kobo

5. Smashwords

6. Google Play Books

Publisher

JD-Biz Corp

P O Box 374

Mendon, Utah 84325

http://www.jd-biz.com/

www.ingramcontent.com/pod-product-compliance
Lightning Source LLC
Chambersburg PA
CBHW070845290526
45795CB00002B/989